MW01514434

Thirteen Days in Psalm 23

in

Psalm 23

CHARLES MOORE

Note From the Writer:

Thank you for allowing me a little poetic license. I have not always capitalized "shepherd" (and related pronouns) on these pages, not because I've forgotten that my Shepherd is Jesus – but because I've written some of the devotional material herein from the perspective of a sheep who understands the shepherd only in part. In fact, I think that's what it means to be a sheep. Along the way, may you and I journey to a fuller knowledge of Christ.

© 2023 Charles Moore . All rights reserved. No part of this publication may be reproduced, distributed, or transmitted in any form or by any means, including photocopying, recording, or other electronic or mechanical methods, without the prior written permission of the publisher, except in the case of brief quotations embodied in critical reviews and certain other noncommercial uses permitted by copyright law.

ISBN 979-8-35091-976-9

Dedicated to Eileen … my lovely bride, best friend, and faithful partner in life and ministry.

And dedicated to the saints of God known as Green Hills Community Church of Nashville, who have welcomed us and loved us as their own.

You're invited
to embark on a 13-day journey.

It's a journey through Psalm 23. It should be a remarkable journey, and I pray for you nothing less!

On this journey, we will become very familiar with one the most beloved psalms in the Bible. Rather uniquely, Psalm 23 has resonated through centuries of Jewish and Christian worship. Sometimes, however, I fear that we have grown so familiar with this psalm that we've stopped being overwhelmed by its beauty. That's why I'm inviting you to seize the opportunity to read through it one small step at a time – much like a sheep takes one small step at a time.

Before David became the king of Israel, he was a shepherd. You may remember that, as a young boy, David was assigned to care for his father's sheep. So, based upon his personal experience as a protector of his father's precious flock, David has written for us a song describing God's gracious relationship to *us*. God is our shepherd and we – God's people – are His sheep. That's what it means to be *in Christ*.

Like other psalms, Psalm 23 is a song of praise. It cries out to God, with a heart of profound thanksgiving, because He cares so perfectly for each one of us. And it points wonderfully to the glorious gospel – the good news – of Jesus because ultimately this psalm was written by the God who has come to save us from our sin.

Without Christ's sacrifice for us, you and I were without hope – like sheep without a shepherd.

I'm so glad we have a shepherd.

This journey through Psalm 23 is a devotional, a Bible study, and a journal of personal response. Each of the thirteen days, I urge you to begin with prayer. Ask God to grant you wisdom and insight into His holy Word. As you take each step, you will have an opportunity to reflect on the passage for that day. Go as deep as you want. Finally, ask yourself: "How is God calling me, in new ways, to understand who He really is – and to worship Him for who He really is?"

After all, the best place to be in the universe is the place where we've been found by God – our faithful Shepherd.

Pastor Charles Moore

Psalm 23

A Psalm of David.

The Lord is my shepherd; I shall not want.
　　He makes me lie down in green pastures.
He leads me beside still waters.
　　He restores my soul.
He leads me in paths of righteousness
　　for his name's sake.
Even though I walk through the valley of the shadow of death,
　　I will fear no evil,
for you are with me;
　　your rod and your staff,
　　they comfort me.
You prepare a table before me
　　in the presence of my enemies;
you anoint my head with oil;
　　my cup overflows.
Surely goodness and mercy shall follow me
　　all the days of my life,
and I shall dwell in the house of the Lord
　　forever.[1]

1 The Holy Bible, English Standard Version. ESV® Text Edition: 2016. Copyright © 2001 by Crossway Bibles, a publishing ministry of Good News Publishers.

DAY 1

"THE LORD IS MY SHEPHERD."

That makes me, yes, a sheep. One of the flock. Sometimes foolish. Sometimes a frolicker. Sometimes fragile.

I tend to stray. I'm prone to wander. I find myself chasing after things that seem attractive, while seldom realizing how far I've gotten off-course. Shiny things have tricked me more than once.

I can be a bit gullible. I don't always learn from my mistakes.

I'm sometimes not so sure that my shepherd has time for me. After all, there are plenty of troubled sheep who need his care. But he finds me every time. It's like I'm the only one on his mind.

So I never get to be the hero of the story, but that's O.K., because my shepherd is the hero. He's the rescuer of all rescuers. He's the friend I didn't even know I needed.

He seems perfectly determined to do what's best for me. Always willing to set aside his own comfort, his strength is displayed in his sacrifice. It must be in his blood.

Day 1: Digging Deeper

"The Lord is my shepherd."

A Bible passage can have multiple practical applications, but it has only *one* intended meaning – and that's what I'm seeking. In my initial observation of this portion of Psalm 23, here's a key word or two that catches my eye …

It's a good idea to see if there are other passages of Scripture where my key words are found. This helps me unlock the true meaning of the words. After having done any research necessary to understand my key words, here's what I've observed …

As a general rule for all Bible study, I want to understand the context of Scripture. Regarding this passage, I want to learn how this passage fits into Psalm 23, and how Psalm 23 fits into the entirety of the Bible. Now, considering the "big picture" of the Bible, here's what I've learned …

A very helpful principle for correct Bible interpretation is: "Let Scripture interpret Scripture." Here are some other Bible passages which I've discovered that can help me correctly interpret this portion of Psalm 23 …

It's always important to relate every passage to the gospel – to the good news of Jesus Christ! Here's how I see Christ in this passage …

Day 1: My Personal Response

"The Lord is my shepherd."

How can I know that God is my shepherd?

Does my being a sheep mean that I am dependent, or that I am independent?

"The Lord is my shepherd." What does this one simple statement teach me about God's love for me?

How is God calling me, in new ways, to understand who He really is – and to worship Him for who he really is?

DAY 2

"I SHALL NOT WANT."

I must be created with a natural bent toward, "How does this thing work?" Always a bit curious. Often sticking my nose where it doesn't belong. Admittedly, sheep-like. Yep, that's me.

At the same time, this sense of wonder is marvelous and thrilling. It stirs my soul, inspires me to explore, and helps me create. It makes me want to try new things, but it also makes me want new stuff. And surprisingly, when I get new stuff, it's not too long before I want more new stuff.

It's hard to stay satisfied. I've noticed that it's hard for all of us to live in contentment, even when we seem to have everything we need.

I must admit: I have everything I need. In fact, there must be a hand of provision that I simply cannot see, because genuine goodness keeps chasing after me. The more I think about it, somebody's taking excellent care of me.

He must be wise.

He must be good.

Sakes alive! I'll bet he outshines every power in the universe ... like a bright morning star.

Day 2: Digging Deeper

"I shall not want."

A Bible passage can have multiple practical applications, but it has only *one* intended meaning – and that's what I'm seeking. In my initial observation of this portion of Psalm 23, here's a key word or two that catches my eye …

It's a good idea to see if there are other passages of Scripture where my key words are found. This helps me unlock the true meaning of the words. After having done any research necessary to understand my key words, here's what I've observed …

As a general rule for all Bible study, I want to understand the context of Scripture. Regarding this passage, I want to learn how this passage fits into Psalm 23, and how Psalm 23 fits into the entirety of the Bible. Now, considering the "big picture" of the Bible, here's what I've learned …

A very helpful principle for correct Bible interpretation is: "Let Scripture interpret Scripture." Here are some other Bible passages which I've discovered that can help me correctly interpret this portion of Psalm 23 …

It's always important to relate every passage to the gospel – to the good news of Jesus Christ! Here's how I see Christ in this passage …

Day 2: My Personal Response

"I shall not want."

How do my curiosity and my creativity work together? How do they reflect, albeit imperfectly, the nature and character of my Creator?

Do I find it difficult to be satisfied? Why or why not?

Jesus taught us to pray (Matthew 6:11): "Give us this day our daily bread." Why?

How is God calling me, in new ways, to understand who He really is – and to worship Him for who he really is?

DAY 3

"HE MAKES ME LIE DOWN IN GREEN PASTURES."

I didn't even know what I was looking for!

But my shepherd certainly did. And he took me there. I did not fully understand the sacrifice that he had made to put me in such a perfect place, but I was there, nonetheless. The land of promise, as far as the eye can see.

He says to me, "Take and eat." It tastes like the bread of heaven.

He says to me, "Take and drink." Wondrously, I thirst no more.

My shepherd seems to know my needs better than I. As if he were himself my food and drink, he supplies sufficiently for each new day. There's more than enough.

He fights my every battle, as if it were his own. And, after he has held the ravenous wolves at bay, my shepherd beckons with grace: "Come to me."

And I come.

I am learning to trust his hand. And I am learning that, behind such a generous hand, there must be a generous heart.

At the end of the day, I can rest secure. Each and every day. And I need not worry about tomorrow ... because my shepherd is already there.

Day 3: Digging Deeper

"He makes me lie down in green pastures."

A Bible passage can have multiple practical applications, but it has only *one* intended meaning – and that's what I'm seeking. In my initial observation of this portion of Psalm 23, here's a key word or two that catches my eye …

It's a good idea to see if there are other passages of Scripture where my key words are found. This helps me unlock the true meaning of the words. After having done any research necessary to understand my key words, here's what I've observed …

As a general rule for all Bible study, I want to understand the context of Scripture. Regarding this passage, I want to learn how this passage fits into Psalm 23, and how Psalm 23 fits into the entirety of the Bible. Now, considering the "big picture" of the Bible, here's what I've learned …

A very helpful principle for correct Bible interpretation is: "Let Scripture interpret Scripture." Here are some other Bible passages which I've discovered that can help me correctly interpret this portion of Psalm 23 …

It's always important to relate every passage to the gospel – to the good news of Jesus Christ! Here's how I see Christ in this passage …

Day 3: My Personal Response

"He makes me lie down in green pastures."

Does God ever rest?

What are some of the things that keep me from resting as I should? Do I ever need someone to make me lie down?

How is my resting related to my relationship to God? Hebrews 4:9 says that "there remains a Sabbath rest for the people of God." How is Jesus my Sabbath rest?

How is God calling me, in new ways, to understand who He really is – and to worship Him for who he really is?

DAY 4

"HE LEADS ME BESIDE STILL WATERS."

He knows where I need to be.

And why.

And when.

He can part the sea.

He can calm the storm.

He makes streams in the desert.

He will satisfy my deepest thirst, and supply my every need.

My Shepherd is the Lamb of God!

Though I am prone to wander, He will lead me home.

Safely home.

I can rest. Now.

He. Leads. Me.

Day 4: Digging Deeper

"He leads me beside still waters."

A Bible passage can have multiple practical applications, but it has only *one* intended meaning – and that's what I'm seeking. In my initial observation of this portion of Psalm 23, here's a key word or two that catches my eye …

It's a good idea to see if there are other passages of Scripture where my key words are found. This helps me unlock the true meaning of the words. After having done any research necessary to understand my key words, here's what I've observed …

As a general rule for all Bible study, I want to understand the context of Scripture. Regarding this passage, I want to learn how this passage fits into Psalm 23, and how Psalm 23 fits into the entirety of the Bible. Now, considering the "big picture" of the Bible, here's what I've learned …

A very helpful principle for correct Bible interpretation is: "Let Scripture interpret Scripture." Here are some other Bible passages which I've discovered that can help me correctly interpret this portion of Psalm 23 …

It's always important to relate every passage to the gospel – to the good news of Jesus Christ! Here's how I see Christ in this passage …

"He leads me beside still waters."

Why do I need a Shepherd to take me to a source of water?

Why does it matter if the waters around me are still? Can God do anything to help me if the waters are rough and turbulent? What can God do?

Read John 4:1-29. Jesus told the Samaritan woman at the well that He could give her "living water." What did He mean? Who can receive this living water? Is this water available to me?

How is God calling me, in new ways, to understand who He really is – and to worship Him for who he really is?

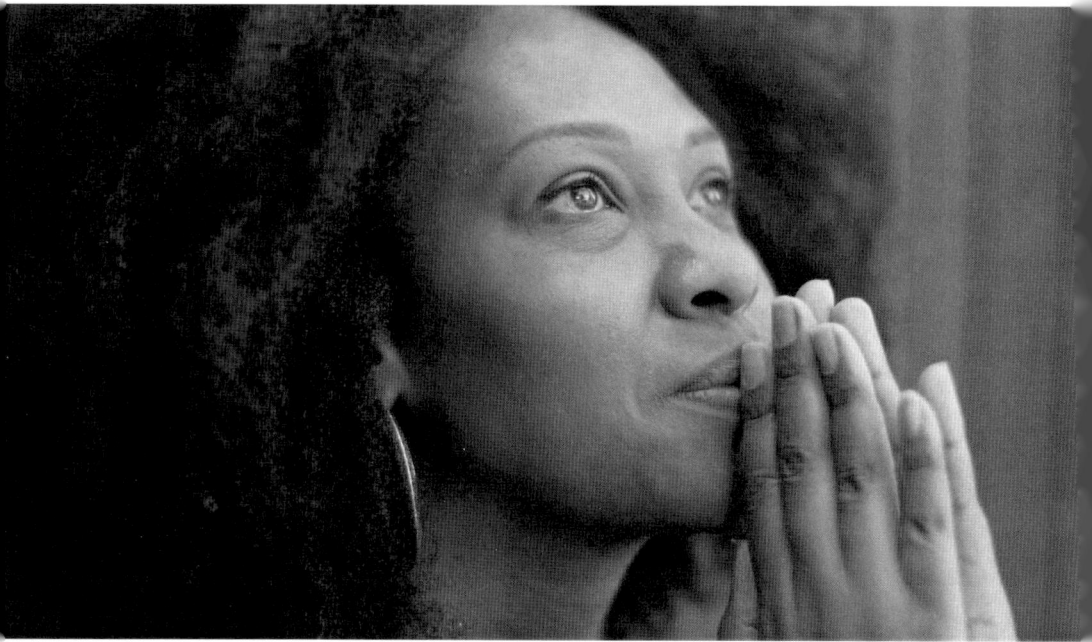

DAY 5

"HE RESTORES MY SOUL."

It doesn't take me long, but the process by which I wander away from truth and joy is subtle enough that I barely notice. I've grown cold. Indifferent. Self-satisfied. Unmoved by what once was the wonder of my first love.

But God! My Shepherd knows my need and my emptiness. He knows the lovely longings that have been ravaged by idolatrous ones. A marvelous Shepherd is Christ! He shepherds on ...

Reaching out to me with awareness that He is as near as my breath. Pouring into me reminders of His unflinching fidelity. Prodding me with His rod of stubborn mercy. A poke that stings but feels strangely endearing, as I am not alone. Changing my course with His staff. A jolt with the force of a whirlwind, yet one which brings comfort at last, for HE IS WITH ME. The rescuer par excellence, Jesus.

I'm often the last to know that I need such divine intervention. Praise God! He's the initiator of every such blessing. I simply receive. All of grace.

He. Restores. My. Soul.

Day 5: Digging Deeper

"He restores my soul."

A Bible passage can have multiple practical applications, but it has only *one* intended meaning – and that's what I'm seeking. In my initial observation of this portion of Psalm 23, here's a key word or two that catches my eye …

It's a good idea to see if there are other passages of Scripture where my key words are found. This helps me unlock the true meaning of the words. After having done any research necessary to understand my key words, here's what I've observed …

As a general rule for all Bible study, I want to understand the context of Scripture. Regarding this passage, I want to learn how this passage fits into Psalm 23, and how Psalm 23 fits into the entirety of the Bible. Now, considering the "big picture" of the Bible, here's what I've learned …

A very helpful principle for correct Bible interpretation is: "Let Scripture interpret Scripture." Here are some other Bible passages which I've discovered that can help me correctly interpret this portion of Psalm 23 …

It's always important to relate every passage to the gospel – to the good news of Jesus Christ! Here's how I see Christ in this passage …

Day 5: My Personal Response

"He restores my soul."

Do I ever need my soul restored? How can I know that I have this need?

In me, what would a restored soul look like?

How does the Word of God relate to my need for a restored soul?

How is God calling me, in new ways, to understand who He really is – and to worship Him for who he really is?

DAY 6

"HE LEADS ME IN PATHS OF RIGHTEOUSNESS FOR HIS NAME'S SAKE."

I think I know the way forward, but my vision is finite and fallible. Purpose and direction aren't really my strong suits. On my best days, I can be a circular wanderer, the last to know that I'm getting nowhere. And there are days when I can't even see over the next hill ... but I know who can.

My shepherd is my sentinel. Gentle, lowly, mighty, victorious. He lives to guard me, and to guide me. Though I meander close to the edge, he never lets me fall beyond his grasp.

The wolves that would destroy me are no match for my shepherd. He is far wiser than their deceptions, and he diverts me regularly. A swift push in another direction. Followed by a definitive pull, if required. Often I don't even appreciate those diversions, as "Foolishness" could be my middle name.

My shepherd seems to know me better than I know myself.

My soul leaps when I hear his voice! That steadying sound is unmistakable in my ear. My shepherd's voice in my ear: that's more than enough for me.

At times, the climb feels steep. The ground beneath me, uncertain. But, right when I need it, peculiar light falls upon my path. He who illumines the stars is leading me, along a road of goodness that I never deserved, safely home.

"He leads me in paths of righteousness for his name's sake."

A Bible passage can have multiple practical applications, but it has only *one* intended meaning – and that's what I'm seeking. In my initial observation of this portion of Psalm 23, here's a key word or two that catches my eye …

It's a good idea to see if there are other passages of Scripture where my key words are found. This helps me unlock the true meaning of the words. After having done any research necessary to understand my key words, here's what I've observed …

As a general rule for all Bible study, I want to understand the context of Scripture. Regarding this passage, I want to learn how this passage fits into Psalm 23, and how Psalm 23 fits into the entirety of the Bible. Now, considering the "big picture" of the Bible, here's what I've learned …

A very helpful principle for correct Bible interpretation is: "Let Scripture interpret Scripture." Here are some other Bible passages which I've discovered that can help me correctly interpret this portion of Psalm 23 …

It's always important to relate every passage to the gospel – to the good news of Jesus Christ! Here's how I see Christ in this passage …

Day 6: My Personal Response

"He leads me in paths of righteousness for his name's sake."

Do I ever wander like a sheep? What's the farthest I've ever wandered? Have I ever been completely lost?

How will I know when I am on a righteous path? What makes the path righteous?

Do I find God, or does God find me?

How is God calling me, in new ways, to understand who He really is - and to worship Him for who he really is?

DAY 7

"EVEN THOUGH I WALK THROUGH THE VALLEY OF THE SHADOW OF DEATH, I WILL FEAR NO EVIL."

God is in my shadowy journey. In the parts of life where not church bells, but alarm bells, ring. Noisy sirens. In the parts that make no sense. In the parts where hope slowly fades ... even the jarring noise gets blurry.

The valley is long. Heaven seems dreamy, but distant. I remember promises, but I can't seem to remember the happy tune with which they were once sung.

One step. Another. Then another. I suppose there's purpose in the pain, but it seems lost. Lost on me. Does that mean I am lost?

Shepherd, draw close. Is that you? Is that You?

Another small step. It doesn't feel like a step of faith; it feels barely like a step at all.

But.

Where there is shadow, there must be light.

"Even though I walk through the valley of the shadow of death, I will fear no evil."

A Bible passage can have multiple practical applications, but it has only *one* intended meaning – and that's what I'm seeking. In my initial observation of this portion of Psalm 23, here's a key word or two that catches my eye …

It's a good idea to see if there are other passages of Scripture where my key words are found. This helps me unlock the true meaning of the words. After having done any research necessary to understand my key words, here's what I've observed …

As a general rule for all Bible study, I want to understand the context of Scripture. Regarding this passage, I want to learn how this passage fits into Psalm 23, and how Psalm 23 fits into the entirety of the Bible. Now, considering the "big picture" of the Bible, here's what I've learned …

A very helpful principle for correct Bible interpretation is: "Let Scripture interpret Scripture." Here are some other Bible passages which I've discovered that can help me correctly interpret this portion of Psalm 23 …

It's always important to relate every passage to the gospel – to the good news of Jesus Christ! Here's how I see Christ in this passage …

Day 7: My Personal Response

"Even though I walk through the valley of the shadow of death, I will fear no evil."

Have I ever found myself in the valley of the shadow of death? In the future, should I expect to find myself in the valley of the shadow of death?

What is the connection between fear and sadness? Between fear and despair?

What are my deepest fears today? Does Christ have anything to say to me about those fears?

How is God calling me, in new ways, to understand who He really is – and to worship Him for who he really is?

DAY 8

"FOR YOU ARE WITH ME; YOUR ROD AND YOUR STAFF, THEY COMFORT ME."

As I make my way along this winding road, I often need a tug of redirection. The surprising touch of his merciful rebuke is his kindness in disguise. The crook may startle me as it swiftly catches my stubborn neck, but eventually it reminds me that my shepherd left all the others to come find me. Me.

That rod that he carries speaks loudly as unquestionable authority, and it is, but behind it is a wide smile of approval. We are not strangers, and I am his. I belong. Even my shepherd's discipline is grace.

So we move along. We. He and I. Like friends. Sometimes, he carries me.

The sunshine won't last forever, a reality that I seem to keep forgetting. But he knows about tomorrow, and he never forgets. He always sees the bigger picture, and he keeps getting me where I need to be. In fact, he's always preparing a place for me.

Yes, those storm clouds do roll in. They turn dark and threatening, and I grow fearful and even terrified. I forget in whom I'm trusting. Where's that certain rod ... and where's that steady staff?

But, as I make my way around every bend, I am never alone! Like the famous painter, I'm included in the greatest love story that has ever been written or told. My name may be unknown to most, but it's permanently engraved in a book that will never fade. And, within that great adventure which is still unfolding before my very eyes, I am never alone.

Day 8: Digging Deeper

"For you are with me; your rod and your staff, they comfort me."

A Bible passage can have multiple practical applications, but it has only *one* intended meaning – and that's what I'm seeking. In my initial observation of this portion of Psalm 23, here's a key word or two that catches my eye …

It's a good idea to see if there are other passages of Scripture where my key words are found. This helps me unlock the true meaning of the words. After having done any research necessary to understand my key words, here's what I've observed …

As a general rule for all Bible study, I want to understand the context of Scripture. Regarding this passage, I want to learn how this passage fits into Psalm 23, and how Psalm 23 fits into the entirety of the Bible. Now, considering the "big picture" of the Bible, here's what I've learned …

A very helpful principle for correct Bible interpretation is: "Let Scripture interpret Scripture." Here are some other Bible passages which I've discovered that can help me correctly interpret this portion of Psalm 23 …

It's always important to relate every passage to the gospel – to the good news of Jesus Christ! Here's how I see Christ in this passage …

Day 8: My Personal Response

"For you are with me; your rod and your staff, they comfort me."

If God is truly with me, does that mean that I am never alone? Is it possible for me to feel alone even when I'm not alone?

What is the meaning of "Immanuel"? Where in the Bible do I find this word? To whom, precisely, does this important title refer?

What is the connection between God's discipline and His love?

How is God calling me, in new ways, to understand who He really is – and to worship Him for who he really is?

DAY 9

"YOU PREPARE A TABLE BEFORE ME IN THE PRESENCE OF MY ENEMIES."

With so much danger in the world, and so much uncertainty, how can we enjoy anything?

We are tired. Our energy has been zapped. Even the thought of a quick bite seems overwhelming. And yet ...

This time, there will be no drive-thru service. Instead, a feast has been spread before us. We will delight in only the best of fare, and the delights will be served by the very best of hands.

Hands that welcome prodigals. Hands that bless little children. Hands that touch blinded eyes and outcast lepers. Hands that embrace enemies until they are friends.

Hands with nail scars.

With us, the Bread of Life is willing to break bread. We have no ordinary host, and the table is set.

"You prepare a table before me in the presence of my enemies."

A Bible passage can have multiple practical applications, but it has only *one* intended meaning - and that's what I'm seeking. In my initial observation of this portion of Psalm 23, here's a key word or two that catches my eye ...

It's a good idea to see if there are other passages of Scripture where my key words are found. This helps me unlock the true meaning of the words. After having done any research necessary to understand my key words, here's what I've observed ...

As a general rule for all Bible study, I want to understand the context of Scripture. Regarding this passage, I want to learn how this passage fits into Psalm 23, and how Psalm 23 fits into the entirety of the Bible. Now, considering the "big picture" of the Bible, here's what I've learned ...

A very helpful principle for correct Bible interpretation is: "Let Scripture interpret Scripture." Here are some other Bible passages which I've discovered that can help me correctly interpret this portion of Psalm 23 ...

It's always important to relate every passage to the gospel - to the good news of Jesus Christ! Here's how I see Christ in this passage ...

Day 9: My Personal Response

"You prepare a table before me in the presence of my enemies."

Jesus called Himself "the bread of life" (John 6:35). What difference does this make to me?

Is it possible for my enemies to derail God's plan for my life? How does God feel toward my enemies? How should I feel toward my enemies?

How do I know that Christ has invited me to sit at His table? Where is this table? Who else can sit at this table? Who else has been invited to sit at this table?

How is God calling me, in new ways, to understand who He really is – and to worship Him for who he really is?

DAY 10

"YOU ANOINT MY HEAD WITH OIL."

When Moses met God on Sinai, he came back with a sacred recipe: cassia, cinnamon, myrrh, and olive oil. This mixture would anoint both things and people, and the oil would consecrate, heal, and comfort. Much later, James would tell the church to use oil in praying for the sick.

And God, our gracious Father, anoints us.

He has sealed me with His Spirit, much like a dad assures his child that all will be well. The perfume of Christ's perfections renews and refreshes my wayward soul. Even in the battleground that is my mind, I find rest in Him.

Here within the sound of His voice, such joy!

The war feels not yet over, but I hear already the sounds of victory. Sing along, o my soul! There's a distinct mix of merry even in these salty tears. For the Lord is, indeed, my Shepherd!

"You anoint my head with oil."

A Bible passage can have multiple practical applications, but it has only *one* intended meaning – and that's what I'm seeking. In my initial observation of this portion of Psalm 23, here's a key word or two that catches my eye …

It's a good idea to see if there are other passages of Scripture where my key words are found. This helps me unlock the true meaning of the words. After having done any research necessary to understand my key words, here's what I've observed …

As a general rule for all Bible study, I want to understand the context of Scripture. Regarding this passage, I want to learn how this passage fits into Psalm 23, and how Psalm 23 fits into the entirety of the Bible. Now, considering the "big picture" of the Bible, here's what I've learned …

A very helpful principle for correct Bible interpretation is: "Let Scripture interpret Scripture." Here are some other Bible passages which I've discovered that can help me correctly interpret this portion of Psalm 23 …

It's always important to relate every passage to the gospel – to the good news of Jesus Christ! Here's how I see Christ in this passage …

Day 10: My Personal Response

"You anoint my head with oil."

The Bible says that followers of Christ have been "anointed by the Holy One" (1 John 2:20). Who is the Holy One? What does this promise mean for me?

How is my mind a constant battleground? Is it possible for me to experience grief and joy at the same time?

As one who has been anointed by God – if I believe this to be true – how should I view myself? What keeps getting in the way of my viewing myself as I should?

How is God calling me, in new ways, to understand who He really is – and to worship Him for who he really is?

DAY 11

"MY CUP OVERFLOWS."

At times I had no eyes to see the green pastures beneath me. The still waters before me went unappreciated. Yet they were there.

Sometimes I saw the dangers, but mostly I did not. They were ever present indeed, but my Shepherd took the brunt of their fury, while I passed safely by. Shortsighted as I am, I barely noticed or remembered.

His hand was always close, especially when I felt it not. His kindness, real. Even His rod and staff fell on me with the grace of One who is gentle and lowly. His reassuring voice was unmistakable, and calmed my fears, even when I lacked ears to hear. Yet He was relentlessly forceful in His passion for my good.

I wanted my good too, but didn't know that it was already mine! So I went looking for it in ridiculously dumb places. He patiently brought me around. Over and over again, He rescued me from me.

His "no's" were secret blessings.

In every season He has filled my cup. My stubborn cup. Every. Season. Christ drank the dreaded cup, so that my cup could overflow.

Day 11: Digging Deeper

"My cup overflows."

A Bible passage can have multiple practical applications, but it has only *one* intended meaning – and that's what I'm seeking. In my initial observation of this portion of Psalm 23, here's a key word or two that catches my eye …

It's a good idea to see if there are other passages of Scripture where my key words are found. This helps me unlock the true meaning of the words. After having done any research necessary to understand my key words, here's what I've observed …

As a general rule for all Bible study, I want to understand the context of Scripture. Regarding this passage, I want to learn how this passage fits into Psalm 23, and how Psalm 23 fits into the entirety of the Bible. Now, considering the "big picture" of the Bible, here's what I've learned …

A very helpful principle for correct Bible interpretation is: "Let Scripture interpret Scripture." Here are some other Bible passages which I've discovered that can help me correctly interpret this portion of Psalm 23 …

It's always important to relate every passage to the gospel – to the good news of Jesus Christ! Here's how I see Christ in this passage …

Day 11: My Personal Response

"My cup overflows."

How has my Shepherd ever rescued me from me?

Is it true that I have to taste sorrow before I can experience true joy? Why or why not?

In the Old Testament, on more than one occasion, "the cup" is used as a symbol of God's wrath (Isaiah 51:17,22; Jeremiah 25:15-16; Lamentations 4:21; Ezekiel 23:28-34; Habakkuk 2:16). It's used as a similar symbol in the New Testament (Revelation 14:9-10; 16:19). How did Jesus drink this cup for me?

How is God calling me, in new ways, to understand who He really is – and to worship Him for who he really is?

DAY 12

"SURELY GOODNESS AND MERCY SHALL FOLLOW ME ALL THE DAYS OF MY LIFE."

I can't imagine the disasters that have been averted. The dangers that have been held at bay. Though most were way over my head, I think of some of the unwise choices that I've made ... and yet a kind Providence has swallowed up the brunt of the damage ... and left me on a path that I never deserved to find beneath my feet.

How marvelous is grace! Not only were those green pastures and still waters before me, but an invincible army took their post behind me as I traversed every hill and every valley.

Invisible swords. Walls of protection. Chariots of fire.

One has chased me with a love unstoppable. Faithfulness undaunted. Friendship unmatched.

I lie down in safety through not a single merit of my own.

And, when I exhale my last breath along this pilgrim way, my faithful Companion will be unseen no more.

"Surely goodness and mercy shall follow me all the days of my life."

A Bible passage can have multiple practical applications, but it has only *one* intended meaning - and that's what I'm seeking. In my initial observation of this portion of Psalm 23, here's a key word or two that catches my eye ...

It's a good idea to see if there are other passages of Scripture where my key words are found. This helps me unlock the true meaning of the words. After having done any research necessary to understand my key words, here's what I've observed ...

As a general rule for all Bible study, I want to understand the context of Scripture. Regarding this passage, I want to learn how this passage fits into Psalm 23, and how Psalm 23 fits into the entirety of the Bible. Now, considering the "big picture" of the Bible, here's what I've learned ...

A very helpful principle for correct Bible interpretation is: "Let Scripture interpret Scripture." Here are some other Bible passages which I've discovered that can help me correctly interpret this portion of Psalm 23 ...

It's always important to relate every passage to the gospel - to the good news of Jesus Christ! Here's how I see Christ in this passage ...

Day 12: My Personal Response

"Surely goodness and mercy shall follow me all the days of my life."

If I am much like a sheep, does that mean that I know when I am being protected? Do I know when I am being provided for?

Why is it a good idea for me to count my blessings?

Read Romans 8:28. What is the promise of that verse, and how does it apply to me? What kinds of things tend to make me forget this amazing promise?

How is God calling me, in new ways, to understand who He really is – and to worship Him for who he really is?

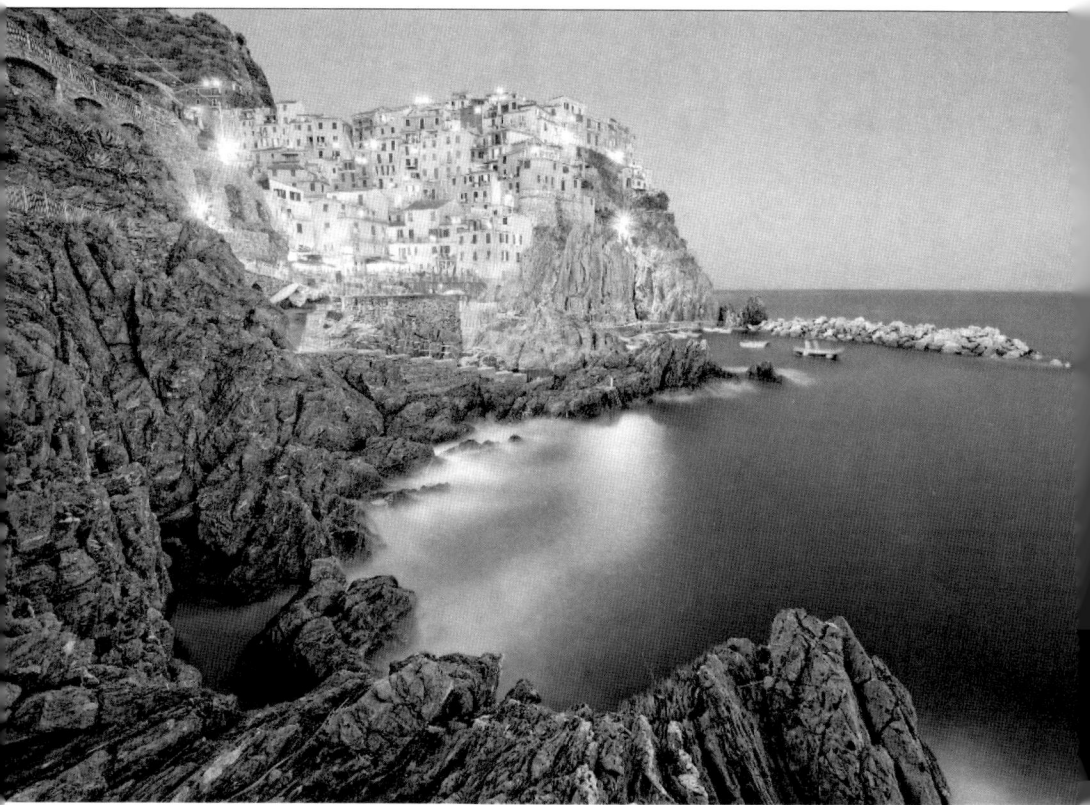

DAY 13

"AND I SHALL DWELL IN THE HOUSE OF THE LORD FOREVER."

My shepherd has a plan for the ages. Why he chose to include me in it, I'll never know. But, hallelujah, I'm in!

On that day, every detour will make perfect sense. Every crooked road will suddenly lead straight to joy. In the twinkling of an eye, every dark and lonesome valley will blossom with vibrant and colorful fruit of eternal beauty.

Sadness will yield to laughter, and the most exhilarating of adventures awaits.

My feet are still here, but my citizenship is out of this world! I can barely conceive of such grace. And it's as good as done.

My shepherd said, "Fear not." So I will take him at his word. His promises are absolutes. He has made certain that death will not win in the end, but it will only usher me into the very best chapter of all.

And, in that grand house, I already have a room. It is bright with the light of my shepherd's face, and the light will never cease to shine. The house is in a city so unbelievably gorgeous that the details can't be captured by any language under heaven.

It must indeed be true: "It is finished!"

Day 13: Digging Deeper

"And I shall dwell in the house of the Lord forever."

A Bible passage can have multiple practical applications, but it has only *one* intended meaning – and that's what I'm seeking. In my initial observation of this portion of Psalm 23, here's a key word or two that catches my eye ...

It's a good idea to see if there are other passages of Scripture where my key words are found. This helps me unlock the true meaning of the words. After having done any research necessary to understand my key words, here's what I've observed ...

As a general rule for all Bible study, I want to understand the context of Scripture. Regarding this passage, I want to learn how this passage fits into Psalm 23, and how Psalm 23 fits into the entirety of the Bible. Now, considering the "big picture" of the Bible, here's what I've learned ...

A very helpful principle for correct Bible interpretation is: "Let Scripture interpret Scripture." Here are some other Bible passages which I've discovered that can help me correctly interpret this portion of Psalm 23 ...

It's always important to relate every passage to the gospel – to the good news of Jesus Christ! Here's how I see Christ in this passage ...

Day 13: My Personal Response

"And I shall dwell in the house of the Lord forever."

What is the connection between hope and fear? Between love and fear?

"Beloved, we are God's children now, and what we will be has not yet appeared; but we know that when he appears we shall be like him, because we shall see him as he is" (1 John 3:2). When I consider that moment, what will it be like?

Do I believe Christ's promise of eternal life? What difference does the hope of heaven make in me? Is my trust securely in the Son of God?

How is God calling me, in new ways, to understand who He really is - and to worship Him for who he really is?

"The position of this psalm is worthy of notice. It follows the twenty-second, which is peculiarly the Psalm of the Cross. There are no green pastures, no still waters on the other side of the twenty-second psalm. It is only after we have read, 'My God, my God, why hast thou forsaken me?' that we come to 'The Lord is my Shepherd.' We must by experience know the value of blood-shedding, and see the sword awakened against the Shepherd, before we shall be able truly to know the Sweetness of the good Shepherd's care."

Charles Haddon Spurgeon, 1834 – 1892